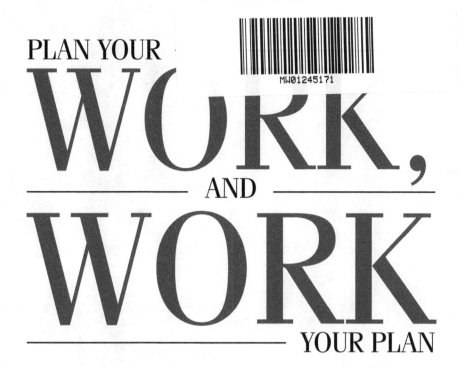

PLAN YOUR WORK, AND WORK YOUR PLAN

REV. DR. FRANCIS TABLA

FOREWORD BY DR. LEO ENDEL

ISBN 978-1-68570-962-4 (paperback)
ISBN 978-1-68570-963-1 (digital)

Christian Faith Publishing
832 Park Avenue
Meadville, PA 16335
www.christianfaithpublishing.com

Printed in the United States of America

Mrs. Marie Yarsiah Hayes
(Photo by Marie Hayes.)

I have decided to dedicate this book to Marie Yarsiah Hayes. I don't know of another woman outside my family who has been so interested in my personal growth, professional development, and ministry development as Marie Hayes has. I dedicate this book to her for the many invaluable services she has rendered me, our church family, and the community at large. Sis. Marie, as she is affectionately called, was instrumental in obtaining a scholarship for my doctoral study at Luther Seminary in Saint Paul, Minnesota. In her role as director of international students and scholar affairs, she has assisted many students from around the world to attend Luther Seminary. Sis. Marie is a native of Liberia, West Africa. Due to the motherly role she has also played in her office, some African students refer to her as Mama Marie, which is a prestigious title and honor in the African context. She is one of my biggest fans. Upon completing my doctoral thesis, Sis. Marie made sure she sat down in the room with the academic panel to give me moral support and to watch me defend my thesis. My family could never be able to repay my professor (as I call her sometimes), but we want her kind gesture to be memorialized perpetually. Sis. Marie, on behalf of the many students from around the world, we dedicate this book to you with much appreciation and deep gratitude! We love you.

CONTENTS

FOREWORD

"Successful people are people who sit down and plan their work and work their plan." Reverend Dr. Francis Tabla has shown us from scripture and experience the power of developing and working a plan.

Dr. Tabla arrived in Minnesota with a God-sized dream and a passion for accomplishing that dream. His dream was a strong and vibrant immigrant church in North America that God could use to touch the world.

Step by step he worked the plan despite detractors and distractions, pitfalls and potholes. In the end, Dr. Tabla led recent immigrants to establish a congregation, buy land, secure loans, and build a facility valued in excess of ten million dollars.

How did God use this man to accomplish so much? He worked hard to discover where his dream was needed the most, and then he painted a clear and compelling vision of a church that would impact the world. Dr. Tabla never took his eyes off that vision. Then he thought through and set the intermediary goals necessary to reach the different stages of development, putting plans in place to reach each intermediary goal. Along the journey, plans were adjusted, but the ultimate goal never changed.

As you read this book, you will gain knowledge from his biblical insights and his practical wisdom. This is not a book in which you get lost in the journey. This is a book that will keep you focused on the task. Tabla's practical wisdom will thus help you to "plan your work and work your plan."

Ebenezer Community Church has fulfilled Dr. Tabla's initial vision that now enables even greater work to be done. While physically building a building, Dr. Tabla has been expanding the leadership base of the congregation. They are now a leadership development center and a church planting network. What was accomplished in brick and mortar is now being multiplied by leaders who will replicate what their founding pastor has done.

By planning his work and working his plan, Dr. Tabla is now touching the world to the glory of God.

Dr. Leo A. Endel, executive director
Minnesota-Wisconsin Baptist Convention
Rochester, Minnesota

ACKNOWLEDGMENTS

Thanks to Marie Hayes for encouraging me to put this teaching into a book form. I was carrying out my responsibility as a pastor to teach and train the flock, but I had no idea the extent to which this teaching was impacting the lives of people. Praise God! Thanks to my Ebenezer Community Church family for assisting with editing the manuscript and for allowing me to share this book in sermon form for years. Thanks to all of you who are already living out the message of this book. God bless you richly.

INTRODUCTION

Plan Your Work, and Work Your Plan is both a workbook and a book to inspire or provoke you to make planning a part of your daily living. The basic purpose of this book is to help you be a person who plans, sticks to the plan, and accomplishes their goals. The book has three chapters. Chapter 1 discusses some ancient planners, namely, God, Jesus Christ, and strangely enough, an ant. Our attention is drawn to how God planned His work and worked His plan, Jesus's attitude toward planning, and how one of the smallest creatures in the world, the ant, plans for survival on a yearly basis. Chapter 2 is about planning your work. Here, I discuss some of the fundamentals related to planning, including goal setting, an acrostic description of SMART, and determining the four Ps to help you accomplish your goals. Chapter 3 discusses working your plan. My argument is having a plan is not enough; you have to work it. Some of the rudiments of working your plan include setting time frames, self-evaluation, being accountable, overcoming distractions, being prepared to make adjustments, and some real-life examples. You are in for a treat! Let's get on the journey!

CHAPTER 1

ANCIENT PLANNERS

God and planning

Our god is a god of plans. When you read Genesis chapter 1, the Bible opens up with the planning nature of God. God first created the universe in a formless and desolate manner (Genesis 1:1–2). God had a strategic plan in place to bring the cosmos out of chaos. God planned what He would do on the first day through the seventh day. You are invited to walk with me very closely, and let us, together, examine God's plan for each day to see whether He accomplished it and what we can learn from Him.

First day

Here is what God *planned* and did on the first day:

> Then God said, "*Let there be light.*" *And light appeared. And God was pleased with it and divided the light from the darkness. He called the light "daytime," and the darkness "nighttime." Together they formed the **first day**.* (Genesis 1:3–5 TLB)

Second day

Here is what God *planned* and did on the second day:

> And God said, "Let the vapors separate to form the sky above and the oceans below. So God made the sky, dividing the vapor above from the water below. This all happened on **the second day**. (Genesis 1:6–8 TLB)

The third day

Here is what God *planned* and did on the third day of His creation:

> Then God said, "Let the water beneath the sky be gathered into oceans so that the dry land will emerge." And so it was. Then God named the dry land "earth," and the water "seas." And God was pleased. And he said, "Let the earth burst forth with every sort of grass and seed-bearing plant, and fruit trees with seeds inside the fruit, so that these seeds will produce the kinds of plants and fruits they came from." And so it was, and God was pleased. This all occurred on **the third day**. (Genesis 1:9–13 TLB)

The fourth day

Here is what God *planned* and did on the fourth day:

> Then God said, "*Let bright lights appear in the sky to give light to the earth and to identify the day and the night; they shall bring about the seasons on the earth, and mark the days and years.*" And so it was. For God had made two huge lights, the sun and moon, to shine down upon the earth—the

larger one, the sun, to preside over the day and the smaller one, the moon, to preside through the night; he had also made the stars. And God set them in the sky to light the earth, and to preside over the day and night, and to divide the light from the darkness. And God was pleased. This happened **the fourth day**. (Genesis 1:14–19 TLB)

The fifth day

Here is what God *planned* and did on the fifth day

Then God said, "Let the waters teem with fish and other life, and let the skies be filled with birds of every kind." So God created great sea animals, and every sort of fish and every kind of bird. And God looked at them with pleasure, and blessed them all. "Multiply and stock the oceans," he told them, and to the birds he said, "Let your numbers increase. Fill the earth!" That ended **the fifth day**. (Genesis 1:20–23 TLB)

The sixth day

Here is what God *planned* and did on the sixth day:

And God said, "Let the earth bring forth every kind of animal—cattle and reptiles and wildlife of every kind." And so it was. God made all sorts of wild animals and cattle and reptiles. And God was pleased with what he had done. Then God said, "Let us make man—someone like ourselves, to be the master of all life upon the earth and in the skies and in the seas." So God made man like his Maker. Like God did God make man; Man and maid did he make them. And God blessed them and

> told them, "Multiply and fill the earth and subdue
> it; you are masters of the fish and birds and all the
> animals. And look! I have given you the seed-bear-
> ing plants throughout the earth and all the fruit
> trees for your food. And I've given all the grass and
> plants to the animals and birds for their food." Then
> God looked over all that he had made, and it was
> excellent in every way. This ended **the sixth day**.
> (Genesis 1:24–31 TLB)

The seventh day

On the seventh day, God *planned* that He would do nothing
but rest:

> And on the seventh day God ended his work
> which he had made; and he rested on the seventh
> day from all his work which he had made. (Genesis
> 2:2 KJV)

As we journeyed through God's seven-day plan, you may have
noticed that the days and planned were in boldface to emphasize
that God planned exactly what He was going to do on each day: He
did it, He measured and evaluated what He had done, and He gave
a thumbs up!

God plans His creation and makes things work as He planned
(the sea, land, sun by day, moon by night, rain, day, night, eight plan-
ets, etc. all work according to God's plan). That is one of the benefits
of planning: things continue to work whether you are present or
not. Several years ago, God gave me the wisdom to set up groups
within the Deacons Ministry of Ebenezer Community Church. For a
First Sunday, each group is responsible for preparing and serving the
Lord's Supper and to execute all other responsibilities that come with
it. The first couple of years were the planning phase, which included
the description of responsibilities and scheduling. The demands of
ministry have made it challenging to review the plan annually, but

the plan is working without having to reschedule every year. The groups remain functional with reminders from the chair of deacons, Deacon Gladys Freeman Fahngon. The number in each group may change as the church calls more deacons. Essentially, the plan is in place, and it is working. Planning will help reduce your workload.

Thousands of years ago, God saw His people suffering in Egypt, and He sat down and put a plan together to deliver them. He pre-determined the *person* He would use to execute the plan. "Person" is emboldened because you will see that planning your work necessitates predetermining the "persons" who will help you attain your goals. In this case, God called Moses and informed him of His plan to deliver His people from bondage in Egypt by sending him to Pharaoh to let His people go (Exodus 3:1ff). There were tumultuous interactions between Moses and Pharaoh, which caused some delays, but the plan eventually succeeded because God and His foot soldier (Moses) were committed to the plan.

Our god is a god of plan not only for Himself and for creation but also for you. He goes to the extent according to Jeremiah 29:11 (GNT) by saying, "*I alone know the plans I have for you, plans to bring you to prosperity and not disaster, plans to bring about the future you hope for.*" The question is, do you have plans for yourself?

When the question "*Who is worthy to break the seals and open the scroll?*" was raised in heaven in Revelation 5:2 (NIV), John the revelator said no one in heaven or on earth or under the earth could open the scroll or even look inside it. The reason was the scroll had the plan, or the blueprint, of what it would take to bring salvation to mankind. The task was going to be arduous; hence, no one wanted to attempt it. The situation was so grave that John began to weep. He wept because he knew that mankind was doomed if the plans in the scroll were not executed. As he wept, there was a tap on his shoulders, and he heard the voice of an elder saying "*Do not weep! See, the Lion of the tribe of Judah, the Root of David, has triumphed. He is able to open the scroll and its seven seals*" (Revelation 5:5 NIV).

If God who created us had to plan, it is incumbent upon us to plan, as well. Let us now consider Jesus and His attitude toward planning.

Jesus and planning

Jesus was a master planner. Here are a few things Jesus had to say about planning: *"If one of you is planning to build a tower, you sit down first and figure out what it will cost, to see if you have enough money to finish the job"* (Luke 14:28 GNT). Or *"If a king goes out with ten thousand men to fight another king who comes against him with twenty thousand men, he will sit down first and decide if he is strong enough to face that other king"* (Luke 14:31 GNT). What Jesus is basically saying is that we must plan our work and work our plan.

Jesus didn't just talk the talk; He walked the talk. He practiced what He taught about planning. He once said to his disciples, *"We must go on to other towns as well, and give my message to them too, for that is why I came"* (Mark 1:38 TLB). In essence, He was saying this is according to His plan. Jesus was very cognizant of His planned mission, so He said to His audience, *"For I have come here from heaven to do the will of God who sent me, not to have my own way"* (John 6:38 TLB). In other words, He was saying "I did not come to carry out My own plans, but the plans of the one who sent me."

On several occasions, Satan tried to distract Jesus from His plans. Satan once said to Jesus, *"If you are God's Son, order these stones to turn into bread"* (Matthew 4:3 GNT). Jesus said, according to His plan, *"Human beings cannot live on bread alone, but need every word that God speaks"* (Matthew 4:4 GNT). Satan said, "Oh, oh! This little guy must know scripture!" Satan elevated his game, using scripture to appeal to Jesus's ego and to derail Jesus's plan. He said, *"If you are God's Son, throw yourself down, for the **scripture says**, 'God will give orders to his angels about you; they will hold you up with their hands, so that not even your feet will be hurt"* (Matthew 4:5–6 GNT). Jesus said, according to His plan, *"Do not put the Lord your God to the test"* (Matthew 4:7 GNT).

Satan acquiesced to Jesus's statement and invited Him up the mountain to see the beauty of this world. He continued, *"All this will I give you, if you kneel down and worship me"* (Matthew 4:9 GNT). My friend and brother Dr. Josef Howard of Harvest Intercontinental Ministries argues that there must be something about worship that the devil was willing to give Jesus all the kingdoms of this world if Jesus worshipped him just for split second. Observe closely: here was Satan (the created), telling Jesus Christ (the Creator) that he would give Jesus the creation that Jesus was a part of creating, if Jesus worshipped him. Wasn't that weird? Why should Jesus worship Satan for what He (Jesus) already owned? One reason we are easily distracted from our plans is that we really don't know who we are. Nevertheless, Jesus's response was as before, "That is not according to My plan." My Mission Action Plan (MAP) says, "*Worship the Lord your God and serve only him*" (Matthew 4:10 GNT). Jesus defeated Satan by simply sticking to His plan. Sticking to your plans will, consequently, bring defeat to your enemies.

There are times when distractions to your plans can emanate from your inner circle and from people you least expect. Jesus's disciples also tried to distract Him. He had sent them to a Samaritan village to plan and prepare for His coming. When the disciples arrived, the Samaritans did not receive them properly. The disciples became furious. They returned to Jesus and said, "*Lord, do you want us to call fire down from heaven to destroy them?*" (Luke 9:54 NIV). Very interesting! Here was a group of disciples who could not heal a little boy with epilepsy (Matthew 17:14–21), but they felt very anointed to call down fire to consume an entire village. Jesus told them that it was not part of His plan, "*For the Son of man is not come to destroy men's lives, but to save them*" (Luke 9:56) KJV). Dr. Miles Jones, my late professor of preaching at the Samuel DeWitt Proctor School of Theology at Virginia Union University, loved this passage of scripture. Dr. Jones would argue that Jesus said to His disciples, "Do you know what the other cities and villages would think of Me when they hear that you called down fire to burn this village? 'Here come the burners,' they would say." Dr. Jones said Jesus refused to be identified as the "the village burner."

Your plan will help to guide you through critical moments and, at other times, also serve as your motivation. When Pilate was interrogating Jesus about His mission, Jesus responded to Pilate by saying, "*I was born for that purpose. And I came to bring truth to the world*" (John 18:37 TLB).

7

When Jesus Christ resurrected, two of His followers were leaving Jerusalem for their village of Emmaus, about seven miles from Jerusalem. On their way, they kept talking about what transpired in Jerusalem.

> Jesus came alongside them and asked, "*What are you talking about to each other, as you walk along?*" *One of them, named Cleopas, asked him, "Are you the only visitor in Jerusalem who doesn't know the things that have been happening there these last few days?" "What things?" Jesus asked. Cleopas and his companion continued: "The things that happened to Jesus of Nazareth," they answered. "This man was a prophet and was considered by God and by all the people to be powerful in everything he said and did. Our chief priests and rulers handed him over to be sentenced to death, and he was crucified. And we had hope that he would be the one who was going to set Israel free! Besides all that, this is now the third day since it happened. Some of the women of our group surprised us; they went at dawn to the tomb, but could not find his body. They came back saying they had seen a vision of angels who told them that he is alive. Some of our group went to the tomb and found it exactly as the women had said, but they did not see him*" (Luke 24:13–27 GNT)

Jesus listened to them patiently and then basically said all this was according to the plan of God, as predicted by the prophets.

Jesus had a plan that was given to Him by God. He adhered to the plan, and it worked. Today, we are beneficiaries of the plan of Jesus. Here is our argument: if Jesus, who is our Savior and Lord, had to work with a plan to carry out His mission, we (His followers) will be treading upon dangerous grounds if we refuse to work with a plan on this journey of life. Just as God has plans for you, Satan also has plans for you. Jesus revealed Satan's plans for us in John 10:10 (NIV): *"The thief comes only to steal and kill and destroy."* If you don't have a plan for yourself, the devil's plan for you will prevail.

Ants and planning

The ant is one of the ancient planners. The ant is so ancient and so deliberate about planning that the Bible takes note of it: *"Go to the ant, you sluggard; consider its ways and be wise! It has no commander, no overseer or ruler, yet it stores its provisions in summer and gathers its food at harvest"* (Proverbs 6:6–8 NIV). Another version says, *"Lazy people should learn a lesson from the way ants live. They have no leader, chief, or ruler, but they store up their food during the summer, getting ready for winter"* (Proverbs 6:6–8 GNT).

Although this text is urging lazy people to learn some poignant lessons from the ants, you can conjecture from the text that ants spend a significant amount of time planning their work and working their plan. The ant realizes that it is going to be very difficult to move around in the winter in search for food, due to the cold weather, unless it wants to risk freezing to death. The ant, therefore, spends time storing up food during the summer in an incredible manner. While others are playing and having a good time, the ant stores sufficient food for the winter and spring seasons. If the ant is this wise and galvanizes the courage to plan its work and work its plan, what about us who are made in the image of God? This book is all about planning, which is so vital to the extent that one of the minutest and most unlikely animals that plans is being highlighted. I heard Bishop David Oyedepo of Nigeria say, "Planning is programing to secure the present and capture the future." Do you want to secure the present? Plan! Do you want to capture the future? Plan!

CHAPTER 2

PLAN YOUR WORK

Your life is divided into four sections: morning (from the beginning to preparation), the afternoon (from preparation to achievement), the evening (from achievement to enjoyment), and midnight (from enjoyment to the end of life). Many of us waste valuable resources, time, and energy because we fail to plan, which impedes our progress because we have no plan for the future. We live by the "one day at a time" adage and avoid one of the key elements to life, which is planning. We are made in the image of God. When we plan our work and work our plan, we are mirroring the image of God in us: if we don't plan, we are an embarrassment to the image of God in us.

As pastor of Ebenezer Community Church in Minnesota, I present this teaching at the beginning of each year due to the increase in membership and as a refresher for those who had heard it previously and may need to be motivated. Some of the members hear this teaching for years in a row before they do anything about it; some are quick to forget or become complacent and need to be motivated. When your life is full of plans and accomplishments, it is a good reflection on the organization and its leaders. This may lead people to inquire, "Which church or organization do you affiliate with?" When they see the similarity between you and the church or organization that epitomizes planning, they may ask, "Who is your leader?" And then you respond, "My leader is [for example] Francis Tabla!" That's very good, right? Come and join me. Let's discuss how to plan your work:

What do you want to accomplish?

In planning your work, you begin by asking yourself the question "What do I want to accomplish?" It is important to first sit down and think about what you want to do. Failure to develop the discipline to sit and think things through leads to impulsivity by spending without planning. It will be to your benefit to sit still and ask God what His plan and purpose for your life is. After determining what you want to do, proceed to the next level.

1. Set your goals

    What are your short-, medium-, and long-term goals?

    a) My short-term goal is (for example: to publish one more book in)
    b) My medium-term goal is (for example: to get my graduate degree by...)
    c) My long-term goal is (for example: to be married by the age of...)
    d) My long-term goal is (for example: to own my business by...)

2. Your goals should be SMART

    When going through this exercise with my family, our son Joshua said, "Dad, your goals ought to be SMART." After inquiring what he meant, he said your goals are to be the following:

    S = specific
    M = measurable
    A =achievable
    R = realistic
    T = timely, or have a timeline

After Josh was through explaining, I thought to myself, *Who's your dad?* What Josh said made a lot of sense to me. At this point, he was teaching me, instead of me teaching him. Josh listens to motivational speakers like Eric Thomas, Les Brown, and others. I will share with you examples of his vision chart later. For now, however, here is a short commentary on each of the letters in SMART:

a) *Specific.* Your goals should not be something that is all over the place. Don't accept life on a "one day at a time" basis. Have a target. I heard Zig Ziglar words: "If you aim at nothing, you will hit it every time." Without a target, you will be approaching life "aimlessly," as my late high school principal Dr. T. Kudah Jarry would say. I attended the Booker Washington Institute in Kakata, Liberia, West Africa. (Go, Tigers!)

b) *Measurable.* Your goals should have the ability to be measured. Every now and then, look at your goal, and measure it to see how far you have progressed toward your goal.

c) *Achievable.* Set goals that are achievable. I learned from Josh that when we set goals that are unachievable, they become a recipe for discouragement. When discouragement sets in, abandonment invariably becomes the next step in most instances.

d) *Realistic.* Let your goals be realistic. Don't plan or talk about purchasing a jet airplane when you don't have a bicycle.

e) *Timely.* Set a time frame or deadline for your goals. Say "I want to do this by this time…"
    It is *very important* to note that your goals should be SMART. When your goals are unrealistic, discouragement sets in when they are not achieved. Sit down, and prayerfully set realistic goals.

3. Determine Four Ps

    After setting your goals, the next step in planning your work is determining the four *Ps* you need:

    a) *Determine the* pillars. Pillars are the things that will help you achieve your goals. They are the stairs, or ladders, to your goal. Some of those are the following:

        i.   *Prayer.* The Bible says we should commit our plans unto the Lord and He will grant the desires of our heart (Proverbs 16:3). Always pray about your plans.
             Prayer is not a waste of time, but rather a saver of time. Prayer also saves you from a lot of unnecessary headaches.

        ii. *Information (ask questions).* Whatever you are trying to do in life has been done by somebody before. Asking questions will prevent mistakes others made when they tried to do what you are trying to do. It will save you from spending time, money, or other resources unnecessarily.

        iii. *Investigate.* Carry out personal investigation.

        iv. *Research.* Research the project you are working on systematically to establish the pros and cons.

    b) Determine the *potholes/pitfalls*.
        The potholes/pitfalls are the obstacles or things that will hinder and undermine the process of achieving your goals. Consider how potholes on a road affect your vehicle. These potholes in question will have

the same effect on your goals. Some examples are the following:

i. *"Good times" parties/playing too much.* Some people are too fond of "good times," parties, playing, and pleasure. Many people are always on the lookout for baby showers, housewarming, wedding receptions, cookouts, etc. They are in anticipation for the weekends to attend these events.

ii. *Laziness.* The Bible says laziness brings poverty and suffering (Proverbs 12:24 and Proverbs 19:15). Some people are very lazy. They expect results without effort. I argue that you should be afraid of lazy family members and friends because after you have struggled, worked hard, and God begins to prosper you, some of those lazy relatives or friends will attempt to seek your downfall or seek to reap the reward of your hard work. Be very careful with lazy people.

iii. *Procrastination.* This is wasting too much time. Some people are anointed procrastinators. Procrastinators are those who are suffering from the disease of always putting things off. These are people who miss a lot of opportunities by wasting time. One reason some people are further ahead of others is they use their time wisely. They simply do not waste time. Growing up, I heard this adage, "Time waits for no man," which I did not understand at that time. It was not until much later in life that the meaning of the adage was understood. William Shakespeare once said, "I wasted time, and now time doth waste me." Don't procrastinate. If you procrastinate, procrastination will procrastinate you.

iv. *Excessive sleeping.* The Bible says too much sleep clothes a person in rags (Proverbs 23:21). This means the person sleeps too much, and as such, they are unable to keep a stable job to earn enough money to buy decent clothes to wear. Have you ever met people who always go around asking a friend or a relative to lend them clothes to wear to an event? Excessive sleep may be a factor.

c) Determine the *person(s)*

Determine the person or persons you will need to help you accomplish your goals. You have to make that determination. When God formulated the plan to deliver the Israelites from bondage in Egypt, God also included, as a part of his planning, whom he would use to execute his plans. The candidate was Moses. Some examples are the following:

i. *God.* Seek God for his blessings on your plans.
ii. *Jesus.* Ask Jesus to help you make it work.
iii. *Parents.* Seek guidance from your parents; they are very resourceful.
iv. *Spouse.* Talk things over with your spouse.
v. *Pastor.* Seek counsel and prayers from your pastor. When God called us to plant a church in Minnesota, we met with our pastor, Rev. Dr. Peter James Flamming of First Baptist Church of Richmond, Virginia. He gave us godly counsel that has become so invaluable to the growth of the church. Today, Ebenezer Community Church is ecumenical in our membership. That is, we have several denominations comprising our membership. This would not have been the case without the wise counsel of Dr. Flamming.
vi. *Coach.* Seek advice from your coach.
vii. *Friend.*—Engage a good friend in conversation to motivate you and hold you accountable. When Ebenezer Community Church was very young,

missionaries would come up to Minnesota from
First Baptist Church of Richmond, Virginia, to
do vacation Bible school for our church. On one
of these trips came my friends Rev. Larry and
Janet Posey. After one of VBS sessions for the day,
we took all the missionaries to see the 4.3 acres
of land that Ebenezer had bought for its future
home. Larry pulled me aside in excitement and
said, "Francis, what do you see on this land?" I
said, "I see a beautiful church building standing
here where the members will celebrate the good-
ness of God through joyful worship, lead unbe-
lievers to personal faith in Jesus Christ and to
become baptized members of the church fellowship, nurture them to become faithful disciples,
equipping them to become effective ministry ser-
vants and training them to become intentional
witnesses through evangelism and missions." I
regurgitated the church's mission statement and
added a little commentary on some of the con-
textualized social ministries we would provide the
community after we built. With his eyes bright-
ening from more excitement, he said, "Francis,
how can you translate what you just explained to
me into picture so that anybody who sees it will
be convinced and moved to support your work?"
Before I could respond, he said, "Find a graphics
designer who will do a good brochure for you."
This was the beginning of Ebenezer Community
Church producing brochures. The first brochure
had a photo of the land, a conceptual drawing of
the building to be built, the purpose and mission
statements, a brief history of the church, and the
programs we were currently doing and hoped to
do. God used that brochure to help raise about

$80,000 for our young church. A friend will help you, motivate you, and give you some new ideas.

viii. *Deacon.* Seek advice or assistance from your deacon. Most deacons are very good at assisting their church members. Some of our deacons helped to proofread and edit the manuscript for this book because they have a great command on the English language. Your deacons will help you.

d) Determine the *power*
Power—the force you need to help you accomplish your goals. Some examples are the following:

i. *The Holy Spirit.* The apostle Paul says, *"I can do all things through Christ which strengtheneth me"* (Philippians 4:13 KJV). The Holy Spirit strengthens us or gives us the power to do things. We have to rely upon the Holy Spirit.

ii. *Courage.* It is the inner strength that you possess. It is there. One of the most dangerous tools the devil uses against us is discouragement. There are times when Satan uses the people who are very close to you to discourage you. Be courageous. You need courage in planning. Brian Dodd shares some light on this in his beautiful article "Benefits of Being Courageous":[1]

I. Courage gives your team (family, church, workmates) security.
II. Courage gives your team confidence. (They borrow from your courage.)
III. Courage gives you the grid/standard of what you say no to.

---

[1] Dodd, Brian. "Benefits of Being Courageous." briandoddonleadership.com, accessed on 4/14/20.

IV.   Courage gives you the opportunity to live with a good conscience.

V.   Courage gives you the platform to attract other strong leaders.

VI.   Courage gives you a *healthy* sense of pride.

VII.   Courage gives you strong boundaries and clear marching orders.

VIII.   Courage gives you increased likelihood of success.

IX.   Courage gives you more influence.

X.   Courage makes you a leader worth following.

Nelson Mandela, former president of South Africa, once said, "*Courage is not the absence of fear, but the triumph over it. The brave man is not he who does not feel afraid, but he who conquers that fear.*"[2] Winston Churchill, former minister of defense and former prime minister of Britain, also said, "Courage is what it takes to stand up and speak; courage is also what it takes to sit down and listen."[3] Be courageous. Don't give up on your dream! The Bible says, "*Wait on the Lord: be of good courage, he shall strengthen thine heart*" (Psalm 27:14 KJV).

iii.   *Determination.* Have the determination that you will pursue your dream to the end.

iv.   *Faith.* You have to believe that it will happen. My definition of faith is seeing a thing happen before it happens.

---

[2] https://www.google.com/search?q=courage+is+not+the+absence+of+fear+quote&oq=&aqs=chrome.0.35i39i362l11j46i39i175i199i362j35i39i362l2j46i39i362...15.-1j1j7&client=ms-android-verizon&sourceid=chrome-mobile&ie=UTF-8 (accessed 4/14/2020).

[3] https://www.brainyquote.com/quotes/winston_churchill_161628 (accessed 4/14/2020).

v.   *Steadfastness.* Your mind is resolute and unwavering on your goals. The Greek word for steadfast is *hedraios.* It means "to sit," "to be immovable," "to be settled."[4] Steadfastness is a necessary element in achieving your goals. There are many people in the Bible who were steadfast, and the apostle Paul was one of them. In Acts 20:17–25, Paul was so steadfast that even in the wake of impending death, he was willing to go and complete the mission God had sent him on (just like Jesus did). David said in Psalm 27:4 (KJV), *"One thing have I desired of the Lord, that will I seek after; that I may dwell in the house of the Lord all the days of my life, to behold the beauty of the Lord, and to enquire in his temple."*

Does the Bible call upon us to be steadfast? Absolutely!

I.   In 1 Corinthians 15:58 (KJV): *"Therefore my beloved brethren, be ye steadfast, unmovable, always abounding in the work of the Lord, for as much as ye know that your labor is not in vain in the Lord."*

II.   In Galatians 6:1 (KJV): *"Stand fast therefore in the liberty where with Christ has made us free, and be not entangled again with the yoke of bondage."*

What are some other biblical examples of steadfastness?

---

[4]   *The New Strong's Exhaustive Concordance of the Bible Greek Testament,* page 26.

I.   Hannah: God blessed her with a son (Samuel) after she had been barren for many years (1 Samuel 1:1–28).

II.   King Josiah: "*He did what was right in the eyes of the LORD and followed completely the ways of his father David, not turning aside to the right or to the left*" (2 Kings 22:2 NIV).

III.   Job: "*My foot hath held his steps, his way have I kept, and not declined. My righteousness I hold fast, and I will not let it go. My heart shall not reproach me as long as I live*" (Job 23:11, 27:6 KJV).

IV.   The three Hebrew boys: "*Shadrach, Meshach and Abednego replied to him, "King Nebuchadnezzar, we do not need to defend ourselves before you in this matter. If we are thrown into the blazing furnace, the God we serve is able to deliver us from it, and he will deliver us from Your Majesty's hand. But even if he does not, we want you to know, Your Majesty, that we will not serve your gods or worship the image of gold you have set up*" (Daniel 3:16–18 NIV).

V.   Jesus: "*And it came to pass, when the time was come that he should be received up, he steadfastly set his face to Jerusalem*" (Luke 9:51 KJV).

VI.   Peter and John: "*But Peter and John replied, "Which is right in God's eyes: to listen to you, or to him? You be the judges! As for us, we cannot help speaking about what we have seen and heard*" (Acts 4:19–20 NIV).

What are the benefits of being steadfast?

The Bible declares that when we are steadfast, we will be rewarded:

A. In Matthew 10:22 (NIV): *"You will be hated by everyone because of me, but the one who stands firm to the end will be **saved**."*

B. In 1 Corinthians 15:58 (NIV): *"Therefore my beloved brethren, be ye steadfast, unmovable, always abounding in the work of the Lord, for as much as ye know that your **labor is not in vain in the Lord**."* KJV

C. In James 1:12 (NIV): *"Blessed is the one who perseveres under trial because, having stood the test, that person will receive the **crown of life** that the Lord has promised to those who love him."*

D. In 2 Timothy 4:7 (KJV): *"I have fought the good fight, I have finished my course, I have kept the faith: henceforth, there is laid up for me a **crown of righteousness**, which the Lord, the righteous Judge, shall give unto me that day: and not unto me only, but unto them also that love His appearing."*

I found that Redeemed Christian Church of Strathmore, Canada, has some insightful thoughts on the steadfastness of Ruth in an article, "Understanding the Power of Steadfastness (Part 2)."[5]

---

[5] Understanding the Power of Steadfastness": www.rccgstrathmore.com (Part 2). Accessed 4/22/2020.

God blessed the steadfastness of Ruth:

A. She found a new Lord (Ruth 1:16).
B. She found a new joy (Ruth 4:10)— she married Boaz.
C. She found a new destiny (Ruth 4:17)—great-grandmother of King David.
D. She found a new glory—she is an ancestor of Jesus Christ (Ruth 4:13–17; Matthew 1:1–6).
E. She found a new faith (Ruth 1:16–17).
F. She found a new love (Ruth 3:10).
G. She found a new lifestyle (Ruth 1:16).

My wife and I have experienced difficulties and endured hardship, ridicule, setbacks, trials, and tribulations in our family, marriage, and ministry. Over the almost three decades of ministry, however, God gave us the grace to be steadfast. In the early days of our relationship, we made this resolution as it pertained to the ministry: *we will serve God whether we have it or not.* This resolution was a necessity because we were teaming up for ministry when our country of nativity was in the midst of a civil war. Things were very tough; we could barely find food to eat. This resolution helped us in doing ministry wholeheartedly whether we had or not, and it still helps us to preach the gospel without compromising, or out of fear that members will stop giving their offering when they hear the truth.

God has continually rewarded our steadfastness, and he still does today! Some examples are the following:

A. In the first few years of marriage, we experienced infertility. We were pastors, praying for others to receive their breakthrough, but we were not having children of our own. We did not complain, saying, "O God, how can you act like this? We are serving you, and we only see you blessing the people you called us to serve. What's going on?" No, we didn't do that. But we steadfastly prayed, trusted, and served God. In the fullness of time, God blessed us with five beautiful biological children. We had to go back to God to ask him not to bless us with any more biological children.

B. God has blessed us with many spiritual children and grandchildren at home and abroad. They watched us labor in the Master's vineyard and have been inspired because they have seen how steadfastness pays off in the lives of their spiritual parents.

C. God blessed us to have and to be the undershepherds of a very beautiful church family (Ebenezer Community Church). The church itself is a testament of steadfastness. We were in the wilderness for about eleven years in an attempt to secure a construction loan. We were steadfast. In the fullness of time, God blessed us to obtain loans to build two phases of our project, amounting to millions of US dollars. People come from far and wide almost on a weekly basis to see what God has done with a group of steadfast people. Ebenezer Community Church is a testament of what God can do in our lives when we are steadfast.

D. God has blessed us with many platforms and opportunities that we would have never had outside steadfastness.

We have many more benefits that time cannot permit us to fit here. We can testify, however, that when you are steadfast, God will bless you! Some of our friends in the ministry including Bishop Wolo and Pastor Della Belleh (Harvest Intercontinental Ministries, Liberia), Rev. Kwaku Owusu and Mama Gloria Boachie (Over Brook AG Church, Philadelphia, Philadelphia), Rev. Dr. Tar-u-way and First Lady Retta Bright (Turner Chapel AME Church, Marietta, Georgia), Rev. Stephen and Pastor Odeltha Cole (Christ Triumphant Outreach Ministries, Brooklyn Park, Minnesota), Bishop Musa Korfeh and First Lady Farmah Jeraldine Korfeh (Harvest Intercontinental Ministries, Houston, Texas), Rev. Julius and Pastor Kula Brent (Hope in Christ Assembly, Madison, Wisconsin), Apostle Sam and Rev. Ruth Carr (Triumphant Christian Living Assembly, Liberia), Apostle Samuel and Rev. Marilyn Kollie (Gates Agape Ministries, Liberia), Rev. Dr. Abenda and Pastor Comfort

Tamba (Zion AG Church, Coffee Farm, Liberia), Rev. Dr. Patrick and First Lady Emma Taylor (Fountain Baptist Church, Richmond, Virginia), etc. can all attest to our claim that God blesses steadfastness. We struggled in the early days of ministry, dealing with hardships and challenges that appeared to be insurmountable. All the ministers mentioned above are excelling today at levels beyond the wildest imaginations of some of those who saw our early beginnings. We were steadfast. Today, God has rewarded our steadfastness!

The benefits you receive for your steadfastness may not be the same as another person's, but you can be sure that God will reward your steadfastness. God will not lie. He said in Hebrew 6:10 (KJV), *"For God is not unrighteous to forget your work and labour of love, which ye have shewed toward his name, in that ye have ministered to the saints, and do minister."* And in 1 Corinthians 15:58 (KJV), he says, *"Therefore, my beloved brethren, be ye steadfast, unmovable, always abounding in the work of the Lord, forasmuch as ye know that your **labour is not in vain in the Lord.**"*

Paul was steadfast, and he was willing to face the future as a gallant soldier without fear. He did not throw in the towel. God blessed the steadfastness of the apostle Paul. He wrote over half of the New Testament, planted several churches, and is esteemed in the body of Christ as the extraordinary apostle.

vi. *Willpower.* Greatest human strength. Get to the place where you have confidence.

You cannot afford to defeat yourself. You must have the willpower and believe you are as good and as capable a person God has made. No low self-esteem, no pity party, no excuses. Go for it, and let God help you succeed. The sky is the limit.

Our son Joshua has given me the permission to share his vision board with you. He provided explanation of his board, as well:

Photo by Josh Tabla

The explanation he provided for his vision board is as follows:

Hey Pops, this is the vision board I had before winning my first conference championship my junior year. I had on it that I wanted to finish in the conference championship, but I also had vision for the person I wanted to be in that time as well. The top left is a picture of me, with the words "BECOMING LEGENDARY" because I wanted to become an ORU legend. Underneath that picture are the Indoor and Outdoor triple jump records, which I yet aspire to break. Near the picture of me is one of a podium, where I wanted to finish on top—"1st in CONFERENCE." Beneath that, I have a picture of someone praying and some words describing how to become the person I wanted to be spiritually—"PRAISE, WORSHIP, MEDITATION, PRAYER, FASTING, READING, LISTENING." Some words I would speak over myself include "[I am] SUBMITTED, DISCERNING, AVAILABLE, GUIDED, PURPOSEFUL, THRIVING."

At the bottom is a picture of the location for outdoor nationals, but nobody reached that Meet since Track season was canceled due to COVID-19. At the top I have a picture of MLKJ, as an example of the power of spoken words: "The words you SPEAK last FOREVER." In the top right corner is Naruto, a character from a show I like, who embodies perseverance and moving others to action because of his undying passion and commitment to his goal, and created strong friendships along the way. I wanted to see that quality in my life as well, so I put his picture there next to the word "BONDS." Beneath Naruto, is a picture of fountain, and I wanted that to portray how I'd interact with others. I first needed to get filled up with God, wisdom, knowledge, etc. and then from a place of fullness I could pour into others around me "Be FILLED, POUR, Be FILLED." And lastly at the bottom is a picture of a lot of money, which I believed and still believe will be my portion if I'm a good steward of what God places in my hands. But I don't only want to be a good steward, but a "MASTER STEWARD." Not only of money, but of time, talent, relationships, and every other resource God places under my care.

If you do not know how to go about setting up vision in pictures that will keep you focused, this vision board by NCAA Division 1 Summit League 2019 indoors and 2021 outdoors Triple Jump Conference Champion, Joshua Tabla of Oral Roberts University, could be of help to you. You have to have a vision to pursue, and planning is an integral part of the process. I once heard Bishop David Oyedepo of Nigeria say "Life without a vision is an adventure in frustration, life without a bearing is a burden. Only those who know where they are going ever get anywhere."

CHAPTER 3

WORK YOUR PLAN

Working your plan is determining how/what you are going to do something and how you proceed with it. It's one thing to plan; it is another thing to determine the how, but the key is actually executing the plan.

1. *Set a time frame.* In working your plan, it is important to set a time frame as to when you want to complete your plan. When you are setting a time frame, be realistic and determined to stick to it. When you are planning, set goals at short range (things you want to accomplish in six months to a year), medium range (things you want to accomplish in two to five years), and long range (things you want to accomplish but take longer than five years). It's important that you divide things up so you keep focused to avoid becoming overwhelmed.

2. *Evaluate yourself.* It was discussed how God planned his creation, worked it out, and evaluated his work at the end of each day: "And God saw that it was good." Self-evaluation is a critical and necessary step in the process. Develop a method to evaluate yourself. It can be a questionnaire, an observation report, or a quality check.

3. *Have others to hold you accountable.* Make sure you have someone to hold you accountable. This should be a person you have a lot of respect for and whom you give the per-

mission to speak into your life, even if it means confronting you on subjects that are uncomfortable. The value this brings to you is incalculable.

4. *Work it out.* A plan does not work just by keeping it lying around. You don't go around telling people "Let me have your attention, please! I want you all to know that I have a plan." So what? You have to work the plan. Be a person of your word. Do what you say you will do. The Bible says, "Faith without work is dead" (James 2:17 KJV). A part of working out your plans includes being willing to put in the mental, physical, and spiritual work. You have to grind, put your hands in the dirt, and work hard. Working your plan also entails seeking for the necessary training to be prepared and well positioned. If you have to go to school, go! If you have to be mentored, humble yourself, and be mentored! Work hard, and God will bless the work of your hands.

5. *Overcome distractions.* Develop a mechanism to help you overcome distraction in working your plan. A good question could be: how will this help me achieve my goals? If what is being offered you, said to you, done to you or passed by you does not add any incentive to help you achieve your goal, you will do well not to take it, or entertain it. Exercise self-control and be patient. Not all that glitters is gold. Some offers are meant to entrap you.

Planning helps to keep you focused. You have to be committed to your plan. Sometimes it may be wearisome, but you have to stick to it. The plan will help to keep you focused on what you want to do.

When God gave us the vision to plant a church, he simply said, "Start a church in North America that will reach out to Liberian immigrants." He said nothing more and nothing less. At that time, Liberia was going through different phases of her civil war, and we thought this was God's way of keeping hope alive for a people destitute by one of the most tragic and barbaric civil wars in modern history. It claimed the lives of about three hundred thousand, or 10 percent, of the population at that time.

We conducted surveys in Atlanta, Georgia; Minnesota; New York; North Carolina; Philadelphia; Rhode Island; and Virginia, respectively. Our survey results and prayer determined Minnesota as the place to plant a church. My family relocated from Richmond, Virginia, to Minnesota in June of 2000. In September of the same year, the church plant was birthed and was called Liberian Community Church, because when God gave us the vision, he specifically said we should start a church that will reach out to Liberian immigrants. We received some criticisms from some of our peers in ministry regarding the name, but we endured the criticisms because we were confident we had heard from God. They said, among other things, "We can't come from Liberia and plant a Liberian church in America." Others said, "We can't come to America and plant an African church." One, in particular, said, "I have asked God to deliver me from the hands of Africans." Well, we had a plan, and it kept us focused.

What our peers did not understand was that God's word to us to start a church to reach out to Liberian immigrants was a church-planting strategy by God to get the core group of people he would use to reach more people. For God to reach the whole world with his saving grace, he had to use a core group of people called the Jews. Abel Taye, my Ethiopian brother who is a field coordinator of Christian United for Israel, says the entire Bible, except the book of Acts and the book of Luke, was written by Jewish people. He said Abraham, Isaac, Jacob, David, Joseph, Mary, and

Jesus were all Jews. God used the Jews over the ages to reach us with the Gospel. Two years into the church plant, the need to change the name of the church emanated from (*within*) what constituted the membership of the church at that time. Nobody from outside needed to tell us what to do. The need became evident when the timing was expedient. We planned, prayed, discussed, and settled on the name Ebenezer Community Church, which is inclusive. Currently, we have ten nations represented in our church family, from Ghana, Guinea, Haiti, Jamaica, Kenya, Liberia, Nigeria, Sierra Leone, Togo, and the United States of America. We have grown from eight people to over seven hundred members, and God has blessed us to build an edifice that cost millions of US dollars.

What our critics didn't realize is that it is God who grows his church, and not us. He may give us ideas and send us out to evangelize in various forms, but ultimately, it is God who grows his church. We had a plan, and the plan kept us focused. Some of our critics are amazed at what has happened to us, and some are trying to give different interpretations to the success they see us enjoy. The simple thing is that we had a plan, and we prayerfully stuck to the plan with all patience and diligence.

Here is another example of how a plan can keep you focused. After starting the new church in Minnesota, we began receiving calls a few years later to plant churches in Liberia. During visits to Liberia, we received the calls with the same message to plant churches in Liberia. While we were campaigning for the building project, others questioned, "Why do you want to build such an expensive church in America and not Liberia?" As time went on, some of our members and a few in our leadership started singing the same song in our ears: "Other Liberian pastors from the United States of America are planting and building churches in Liberia, but we are not doing anything in Liberia." Friends, let me just say this strongly: if you don't listen to the voice of God, your very church members will confuse you. We would listen patiently and respond by saying "We are not other pastors. We have not heard from God to build a church in Liberia." The most we were led to do was to purchase land in different parts of the country, amounting to twenty acres. We had a plan, and our plan kept us focused.

What the individuals asking us to build churches in Liberia didn't understand was that we could not be meeting in a classroom or renting a space in a college and, later, a high school auditorium and then take the financial resources of the church to go and build in Liberia, where our current membership is not. The wise and prudent members of the church would withhold their financial resources because they would think we are either not serious or taking them for fools. We have a son in the ministry who was focused on doing project in Liberia and not where he's based with the ministry in the United States of America. The members of the congregation, therefore, held on to their finances. They were basically saying "We are here and don't have a place of our own, and you are talking about doing project in Liberia?" They held on to their finances.

When our son in the ministry announced a building fund for where the church is based to acquire building for the local church, the people started giving.

Another thing those calling us to build churches in Liberia did not understand was, when our base or capacity here in the United States of America becomes strong, we can build churches in Liberia and in all the nations that are represented in the church, as God enables us. By God's grace, we have that capacity now, and we will be going step by step as we are led by the spirit of God. In working your plan, do not follow the crowd. Do not be influenced by peer pressure. Plan your work, and be led by God to work your plan.

6. *Make adjustments.* There may be times when your plans may not go exactly as you determined. Be prepared to

make adjustments, being guided by God's spirit. When our building project commenced, our plan was to build the full project at once. We tried for years to acquire loan, to no avail. We started receiving suggestions that we should consider doing the project in phases. Suggestions were rejected due to an internal fear that the members of the church would become complacent about proceeding with the second phase. God spoke to me clearly about the matter while studying and reading my Bible in Exodus 23:28–30 (KJV): *"And I will send hornets before thee, which shall drive out the Hivite, the Canaanite, and the Hittite, from before thee. I will not drive them out from before thee in one year; lest the land become desolate, and the beast of the field multiply against thee. By little and little I will drive them out from before thee, until thou be increased and inherit the land."* He said, "Francis, I allowed the children of Israel to take the Promised Land little by little so they could not be overwhelmed by their enemies and be consumed by wild beasts. Go on and do the project in phases." It was a needed confirmation from God. He gave me the assurance to do the project in phases. On the following Sunday, the congregation was jubilant after sharing the plan to pay off the balance mortgage we owed on the land and work toward doing the building project in phases. They were so excited! After service, some of the members shook my hand and exclaimed, "That's what we've been waiting for!" God gave us the wisdom to make use of that momentum by reviving our capital campaign and subsequently paid off the mortgage. We burned the mortgage note on the land in September of 2013, during the thirteenth anniversary of the church. From that point on, we began to prayerfully focus all our energy, campaigns, and financial resources on obtaining a loan to build the first phase. *On May 22, 2015,* about eleven years after we acquired the land, we obtained the loan to build. God gave us the wisdom to first build the fellowship hall instead of the sanctuary.

The first phase of fourteen thousand square feet was completed, and on *May 22 of 2016*, we moved into the building, which included a gymnasium, offices, and classrooms, at the cost of millions of dollars. Upon our moving into the building, God gave us a plan to encourage the congregation to pay off a smaller portion of the loan. With necessary adjustments, we worked the plan for a period of ninety days, which culminated into the loan being paid off in September of 2016, by the grace of God.

Our next plan was to pay off the remainder of the loan, break ground for the second phase construction in 2019, get the construction underway, and dedicate the building during our twentieth anniversary celebration in 2020. We, unfortunately, were only able to break ground, due to problems with obtaining a construction loan, coupled with the coronavirus pandemic. Nevertheless, God miraculously provided us the loan on *May 22, 2020*. The second phase of the building construction, comprising twenty thousand square feet, commenced in August of 2020. The building was completed and dedicated on September 5, 2021, during our twenty-first anniversary celebration.

Key observations from the foregoing narrative are that my fears did not happen, and the members were not complacent with settling only for the first phase. No, no, no! A lot of times, what we are afraid of does not really happen. Fear is another instrument of Satan to keep you hostage and to prevent you from walking right into your destiny. The vision was compelling, and the vision was cast properly. We kept working with a plan, made adjustments as needed, and kept the vision before the membership and our well-wishers on a consistent basis. We did not build the full building at first as we wanted to; we did not build the second phase and move into it in 2020 as we had planned, but we made adjustments due to the prevailing circumstances. Our plan kept us focused, and with God's help, the plan materialized one year later.

There are times when things may not work out as planned, but be prepared to make adjustments while being guarded by the Holy Spirit. There is a saying that "man proposes, God disposes." As we reflect upon the whole experience, we can see that God actually brought out the good for Ebenezer Community Church in the midst of the COVID-19 pandemic. So many things worked in our favor that we cannot list now. My strong belief is that if we had not made the necessary adjustments to our plans, we would not be where we are now. Making adjustments may cause your route to be longer, but with steadfastness, you will get to where you need to be. A few months ago, while I was driving to conduct Bible study and prayer meeting at our new church plant in St. Paul, Minnesota, my normal routes were congested. This caused me to take a much-longer route. My arrival was delayed, but I reached my destination nonetheless. As you work your plan, be prepared to make adjustments to still accomplish your goal.

Here are some examples of my personal life plans in two categories and adjustments made to attain results:

A. Some of my plans before I became a Christian:

    I. My plan for my career—when I was at the age of thirteen, my plans included the following:

        i. Be a marine man (work on a ship to save a lot of money).

        ii. Be a pilot (flying planes will allow me to see many places without paying for air travels).

    iii. Be an Episcopal priest (loved the liturgy of the Episcopal church and was infatuated with the vestments worn by the archbishop of Liberia, the late Dr. George Daniel Brown).

II. My plans for having children

    i. My plan included six children, two steps down from my mother, who had eight children. I made up in my mind that I was not going to run any competition with my mother. She was a brave and strong woman to have and raise eight children.

    ii. I planned to have all my children by one woman because my father has three sets of children and my mother has two sets of children. The challenges I experienced as a stepchild and the many inconsistencies witnessed with the men in my family led to the decision to not be like my parents in this regard.

III. My plan for where I would live when I came to America—to *never* live in the state of Minnesota, United States of America, due to the stories I heard about the snow when I was growing up. My plan was to live in Texas because that was where my father had his military training for the Armed Forces of Liberia (AFL).

B. Some of my plans after I became a Christian:

I. When God called me to the ministry, my plan was to attend the Liberia Baptist Theological Seminary to be trained, commit three to five years to full-time ministry in Liberia, and then travel to the United States of America for graduate studies.

II. My plan was not to leave the United States of America without planting a church for the Lord.

III. To obtain my doctorate degree before or by the age of forty-five.

IV. To write books to help empower people and the body of Christ.

Let us examine some of my plans from the time of growing up to current, which covers a period of about forty-five years.

I. Plans to become a marine man, a pilot, or an Episcopal priest did not materialize, but I became a pastor. Things did not go according to my plans, but I had a plan. God knew my heart and positioned me as a spiritual pilot, according to Bishop Darlingston Johnson of Harvest Intercontinental Ministries. He's right! People get on the plane (the church), and God has given me the privilege to serve as the pilot (the pastor) to help them get to their destinations.

II. Instead of six children as planned, God blessed us with five children: Sam, Josh, Christie, Elijah, and Edward Messenger. It was a few years after we had all our children that the Lord ministered to my heart that the sixth child is the church he called us to plant and pastor.

III. My plan to have all my children by one mother worked out blessedly with all my biological children by Pastor Chris Tabla, my high school sweetheart. God is so good! He delivered me from my fear.

IV. My plan to live in Texas did not work out at all. I instead live in Minnesota, the state where, according to my original plan, I was not supposed to live. I am also a pastor in Minnesota, and here I had three of my five children. Adjustments had to be made to my plan to enjoy the will and blessings of God. Somebody said "Never say never." God, indeed, has a sense of humor.

Now let's turn to some of my plans after I became a Christian:

I. Graduation from the Liberia Baptist Theological Seminary was in December of 1993. Three years and nine months were committed to full-time ministry in Liberia. My family travelled to the United States of America for graduate studies on Monday, September 8, 1997, and arrived at JFK International Airport in New York on *Tuesday, September 9*. Bear this date in mind, as it is only going to get interesting!

II. My plan that, when I came to America to study, I would not leave the United States of America without planting a church for the Lord has happened. God has blessed me to plant *churches*! The first Bible study for the church plant in Brooklyn Park was held on Saturday, *September 9*, 2000, exactly three years after we stepped our feet on the American soil. It is amazing how God works! We have seen him doing this over and over at Ebenezer Community Church. He blessed us with the loan to build our first phase on May 22, 2015. We moved into the building on Sunday, May 22, 2016. He blessed us with the loan to build the second phase on May 22, 2020. We were aiming to dedicate and move into the second phase in May, but that didn't work out. Yes, God honored my desire and my plan to plant a church for him, and he graced me to pastor a church that grew from about eight people to over seven hundred and to provide leadership for a young congregation to complete two building programs worth millions of dollars.

III. My plan was to obtain my doctorate degree before or by the age of forty-five. God was gracious and blessed me to obtain, at the age of forty-three, my doctor of ministry degree in biblical preaching with emphasis in stewardship from Luther Seminary. That also worked out well.

IV. My plan was to write books to help empower people and the body of Christ. This book you are currently reading is my third book. The first book, *My Golden Rule: How Men Should Treat Women*, was published by River City Press in 2010. My second book, *Scrap Racism: The Church's Response to Racism* was published in 2020 by AuthorHouse. Some of my plans did not work out as were planned, but I made adjustments to follow the leading of God. It has been a tremendous blessing to adjust my plans to have the will of God prevail in my life. To this, there are no regrets.

CONCLUSION

God, who created, us is a god of plan. Jesus, who saved us, is a Savior of plan. The ants that live with us are ants of plan. We have to be people who plan. When we plan our work and work our plan, we are acting out the image of God in us. Don't demote yourself by refusing to plan and refusing to work. My seminary professor, the late Reverend Lawrence Hardy, a Southern Baptist missionary to Liberia, always said, "Failure to plan is planning to fail." He is absolutely right. If you fail to plan in life, you are planning to fail miserably in life.

Successful people are people who sit down and plan their work and work their plan. Working your plan also entails seeking for the necessary training to be prepared and well positioned for opportunities. If you want to be a successful businessperson, acquire some training in that discipline. I heard Pastor Jerome Sackor of Philadelphia, Pennsylvania, say once, "It is better to be prepared and not have opportunity than to have opportunity and not be prepared."

In addition to what Reverend Hardy says about failure to plan is planning to fail, I have also concluded based upon my experiences so far that "it is better to plan and fail than to fail to plan."

As you read through this book and the note about the author, you will see that God has blessed me with many opportunities. I am not sure 10 percent would have been possible without planning. Plan, plan, plan, and plan. My heartfelt and sincere thanks to you for taking your time to read through this material. I appreciate you, and my ardent hope is this exercise will help you. Please let me hear from you at Ftabla7@gmail.com if this book has been of some help to you.

God bless you richly.

KEY TO ABBREVIATIONS

AFL: Armed Forces of Liberia
GNT: Good News Translation
KJV: King James Version
MAP: Mission Action Plan
NIV: New International Version
ORU: Oral Roberts University
TLB: The Living Bible

BIBLIOGRAPHY

Dodd, Brian: "Benefits of Being Courageous." briandoddonleadership.com, accessed on 4/14/20).
https://www.google.com/search?q=courage+is+not+the+absence+of+-fear+quote&oq=&aqs=chrome.0.35i39i362l11j46i39i175i199i-362j35i39i362l2j46i39i362...15.-1j1j7&client=ms-android-verizon&sourceid=chrome-mobile&ie=UTF-8 (accessed 4/14/2020).
https://www.brainyquote.com/quotes/winston_churchill_161628 (accessed 4/14/2020).
The New Strong's Exhaustive Concordance of the Bible Greek Testament.
"Understanding the Power of Steadfastness": www.rccgstrathmore.com (Part 2). Accessed 4/22/2020
Good News Bible: Good News Translation, Today's English Version—Second Edition. Philadelphia, PA: American Bible Society, 1993.
The Living Bible Paraphrased: Illinois: Tyndale House Publishers, Inc. 1971.
The Holy Bible: King James Version. Philadelphia: National Publishing Company, 1997.
The New Strong's Exhaustive Concordance of the Bible: Nashville: Thomas Nelson Publishers, 1995.
The NIV Women's Devotional Bible. Grand Rapids, MI: Zondervan Publishing House, 2012.

ABOUT THE AUTHOR

Rev. Dr. Francis Tabla is a native of Liberia, West Africa. He pastors Ebenezer Community Church, which he and his wife planted in 2000 in Brooklyn Park, Minnesota. The church has grown from eight to over seven hundred members. They also led the congregation to build a multi-million-dollar building. He is currently the African outreach coordinator of Christians United for Israel, with over ten million members in the USA. He leads tours to Israel for African and African American pastors and church leaders and hosts Africa Nights to honor Israel in cities across the USA. He holds the doctor of ministry degree from Luther Seminary in St. Paul, a master of divinity degree from the Samuel DeWitt Proctor School of Theology at Virginia Union University, a bachelor of theology degree from the Liberia Baptist Theological Seminary, and a diploma in electronics from the Booker Washington Institute in Kakata, Liberia. Dr. Tabla is gifted by God as an evangelist, pastor, preacher, and teacher. He formerly served as pastor of the Grace Baptist Church in Barnersville, Liberia. He taught at the Monrovia Bible Training Center and the Liberia Baptist Theological Seminary. He was also the director of Living Way Baptist Bible Correspondence Course (ministry of the Southern Baptist Mission in Liberia). A West African missionary to the USA, Dr. Tabla preaches across the United States and does revivals and leadership workshops for churches and parachurch organizations. He has been featured in numerous articles and newspapers and on a few television and radio networks. He is author of *My Golden Rule: How Men Should Treat Women*, published by River City Press, Minnesota, and *Scrap Racism: The Church's Response to Racism*, published by AuthorHouse, Indiana.

In recognition of the impact God has enabled Dr. Tabla to have on the lives of many people at home and abroad, the First Baptist Church of Richmond, Virginia, set up the Francis O. S. Tabla Scholarship Fund at the Samuel DeWitt Proctor School of Theology at Virginia Union University, which is granted yearly to students pursuing the masters of divinity degree. Dr. Tabla is married to his high school sweetheart, Pastor Christine Jallah-Tabla, and their union of twenty-nine years is blessed with five children: Francis Jr., Joshua, Christie, Elijah, and Edward Messenger.

Printed in the USA
CPSIA information can be obtained
at www.ICGtesting.com
LVHW100755250923
759082LV00001B/357

9 781685 709624